WHAT THEY NEVER TAUGHT US

The Miseducation of the Modern-Day Student

Nyasha Chitakure

DEDICATION

To all those who are perspicacious students of life.

Contents

HOW TO READ THIS BOOK

The path to professional and financial success can be challenging and complex, but with the right guidance and resources, it can also be incredibly rewarding. This book is an instructional manual that offers practical advice formatted as step-by-step instruction

CHAPTER 1: FINDING YOUR FIRST JOB

Money is a tool that we all need. The more money/tools you have, the more things you can fix. A job that pays is the easiest source of making money. Applying for your first job can be a daunting task, but with a little bit of preparation and organization, you can increase your chances of getting hired. Here is how you prepare.

Research potential employers: Start by identifying companies and organizations that interest you, and research their products, services, and mission. The best source to find this information is the company website.

Tailor your resume: Create a tailored resume that highlights your skills, education, and experience. Be sure to read the job description and tailor your resume to what the employer is looking for. Another tip is to use action words and quantifiable achievements to make your resume stand out.

Create a cover letter: Even though most companies do not require cover letters, a cover letter is a brief letter that introduces you and your qualifications to a potential employer. Tailor your cover letter to the specific job and company you are applying to. Below is an example:

"Dear Hiring Manager,

I am writing to express my strong interest in the [Job Title] position at [Company]. As a highly skilled [Your Profession], I am confident that my experience, skills, and qualifications make me a strong candidate for the role.

I have [Number of Years] years of experience in [Your Area of Expertise], with a track record of delivering high-quality work and exceeding expectations. I have worked in both large and small organizations, giving me a diverse range of experience that has helped me develop a strong understanding of how to work effectively with different teams and stakeholders.

In my current role at [Current Company], I have honed my skills in [Key Skills]. I am able to [Specific Skill 1], [Specific Skill 2], and [Specific Skill 3], which have enabled me to [Accomplishment or Result]. I am also adept at [Related Skill or Technology], which has allowed me to [Accomplishment or Result].

I am excited about the opportunity to join [Company] and contribute to its success. I am confident that my skills and experience make me a strong fit for the role, and I look forward to the opportunity to further discuss my qualifications with you.

Thank you for considering my application. I look forward to hearing from you soon.

Sincerely,
[Your Name]"

Practice your interviewing skills: Prepare answers to common interview questions and practice your interviewing skills. Be prepared to discuss your qualifications and experience in relation to the job you are applying for.

Follow up: After your interview, send a thank you note to the interviewer and be sure follow up to inquire about the status of your application if the employer has not reached out to you. Below is an example:

"Dear [Interviewer's Name],

I wanted to take a moment to thank you for taking the time to meet with me earlier today to discuss the [Job Title] position at [Company]. I appreciated the opportunity to learn more about the company, its culture, and the responsibilities of the role.

I am particularly excited about the prospect of working with such a talented team and contributing to the success of [Company]. Our conversation only further solidified my interest in the position.

If there is any additional information I can provide or if you have any further questions, please don't hesitate to reach out to me. Thank you again for your time and consideration.

Best regards,

[Your Name]"

Network: It is important to not only rely on job posts, sometimes it is also useful to reach out to people you know who works in the field you are interested in. Ask them if they know about any opportunities, or if they can help you get in touch with someone that may have an opening. Remember, its all about who you know.

By following these tips, you will be well-prepared to apply for your first job and increase your chances of getting hired. Remember to stay positive, be confident, and present your best self to potential employers. Good luck!

CHAPTER 2: PREPARING FOR AN INTERVIEW

Preparing for a job interview is an important step in the process of finding a new job. It allows you to present your best self to the interviewer and to make a good impression. The first interview is usually a 30 minute phone call which is known as a phone screening. During the phone screening, the interviewer will ask a few questions to determine if you are a good candidate to invite for an official interview. Here are some tips to help you prepare for a job interview:

Review the job posting and requirements: Look over the job posting and requirements again and make sure you understand what the company is looking for. You don't want to be surprised when the interviewer starts to describe the job tasks.

Dress appropriately: Make sure you dress professionally and appropriately for the interview. This will show the interviewer that you are taking the interview seriously and that you are professional.

Prepare questions: Prepare some questions to ask the interviewer. This will show the interviewer that you are genuinely interested in the company and the job, and it will also help you to learn more about the company and the role. Below are some questions to ask:

1. *What is the company culture like?*
2. *What are the key responsibilities of the role?*
3. *What are the biggest challenges that the team is facing right now?*
4. *How do you see this position evolving in the next few*

years?
5. *What are the opportunities for growth and professional development within the company?*
6. *Can you tell me more about the team I will be working with?*
7. *What is the company's approach to work-life balance?*
8. *What are the most important qualities for success in this position?*
9. *Can you walk me through a typical day or week in this role?*
10. *How does the company measure success and what are the most important metrics for this role?*

Get to the location on time: Plan to arrive at the location at least 10-15 minutes early. This shows your punctuality and consideration for the interviewer's time.

Common Interview Questions

Here are some common questions that are often asked in job interviews:

1. *Can you tell me about yourself?*
2. *Why are you interested in this position?*
3. *Why do you want to work for our company?*
4. *What are your strengths?*
5. *What are your weaknesses?*
6. *Can you give an example of a time when you had to solve a difficult problem?*
7. *Can you tell me about a time when you had to work as part of a team?*
8. *How do you handle stress and pressure?*
9. *Can you give an example of a project you have led?*
10. *What are your salary expectations?*

11. *Why should we hire you?*
12. *How do you handle criticism?*
13. *What do you know about the company?*
14. *What are your long-term career goals?*
15. *Do you have any questions for me?*

It is important to note that these questions may vary depending on the job you are applying for, the company culture, and the interviewer style. It is always good to be ready for common questions as well as specific ones related to the job you're applying for. Remember that you are also interviewing the interviewer to determine if the company is a good fit for you.

CHAPTER 3: WHAT TO DO AFTER AN INTERVIEW

After a job interview, the wait begins. Be patient but do not hesitate to reach out to the employer for a status update if an unreasonable amount of time has passed. Below is how you can follow up:

"Dear [Interviewer's Name],

I hope this email finds you well. I wanted to follow up on the status of my interview for the [Job Title] position at [Company].

I enjoyed meeting with you and the team to discuss the opportunity, and I remain very interested in the role and the company. I am eager to learn more about next steps and would appreciate any updates you can provide.

Please let me know if there is any additional information I can provide to help with the decision-making process. Thank you again for your time and consideration.

Best regards,

[Your Name]"

Getting rejected

If you don't get the job offer, it can be disappointing, but it's important to remember that it happens to everyone. Here are a few things you can do if you don't get the job offer:

Ask for feedback: If you didn't get the job, don't be afraid to ask the employer for feedback on your interview and why you weren't selected. It's a great way to learn what you need to improve for your next job opportunity. Here is how you can ask for feedback:

"Dear [Employer's Name],

I hope this email finds you well. I wanted to thank you for taking the time to consider me for the [Job Title] position at [Company], and while I am disappointed to hear that I was not selected for the role, I remain very interested in the company and would appreciate any feedback you could provide on my candidacy.

I am committed to continuous learning and growth, and any insights you can offer would be valuable as I look for new opportunities. Specifically, I would be interested in learning more about areas where I could improve my skills or experience, as well as any feedback on how I presented myself during the interview process.

Thank you again for your time and consideration. I look forward to staying in touch and potentially exploring other opportunities to work together in the future.

Best regards,

[Your Name]"

Reflect on the experience: Reflect on the interview process and consider what you could have done differently or better. This will help you to improve your interviewing skills and to prepare better for future job opportunities.

Keep it in perspective: Keep in mind that one job rejection is not the end of the world. Keep searching and applying for jobs. Even if you didn't get this job, there are plenty of other opportunities out there.

Network: Don't underestimate the power of networking. Let your network know that you're still looking for a job and ask for leads, referrals or any other help they can offer.

Networking on LinkedIn

Optimize your LinkedIn profile: Make sure your LinkedIn profile is up-to-date and professional. Highlight your skills, experience, and achievements, and use keywords that are relevant to your target job.

Connect with people in your industry: Look for people who work in your industry or who have jobs that you are interested in. Connect with them and send a personalized message explaining why you are interested in connecting. Here is an example of an initial message to send:

"Dear [First Name],

I hope this message finds you well. I came across your profile on LinkedIn and was impressed by your experience in [relevant field]. I would love to connect with you and learn more about your career journey.

I am currently working as [your current job title] at [company name] and have a keen interest in [relevant field]. I believe connecting with like-minded professionals like you would be a great way to expand my network and gain valuable insights.

Would you be open to connecting on LinkedIn and potentially discussing your experience in more detail? I look forward to hearing back from you.

Best regards,

[Your Name]"

Engage with your connections: Engage with your connections by commenting on their posts, sharing their content, and sending them messages. This can help you build relationships and stay top-of-mind.

Join LinkedIn groups: Join LinkedIn groups that are relevant to your industry or interests. Engage in discussions, share your expertise, and connect with other members.

Reach out to recruiters: Look for recruiters who specialize in your industry or who work for companies that you are interested in. Connect with them and send a personalized message explaining your interest in working for their company. Below is an example:

"Dear [Recruiter's Name],

I came across your profile on LinkedIn and was impressed by your experience as a recruiter. I am writing to express my interest in potential job opportunities that align with my skills and experience.

I am a [your current job title] with [number of years of experience] years of experience in [relevant field]. I have a passion for [relevant skills or industry] and am always on the lookout for new opportunities to grow and develop in my career.

I noticed that your company has a reputation for [insert relevant information about the company] and I would be thrilled to be a part of such a dynamic team. I have attached my resume to this message and would love to discuss potential opportunities with you further.

Thank you for your time and consideration. I look forward to hearing back from you soon.

Best regards,

[Your Name]"

Use LinkedIn's job search feature: LinkedIn has a job search feature that allows you to search for jobs by keyword, location, and other criteria. You can also set up job alerts to be notified when new jobs are posted.

Remember that a job search process is not always easy and it's not uncommon to face rejection, but it is not the end of your journey. Learn from the experience and move forward with a positive attitude and the determination to find the right job for you.

CHAPTER 4: GETTING THE JOB OFFER

Congratulations on getting a job offer! Here are a few things you can do after you receive a job offer:

Take time to review the offer: Read through the offer carefully, make sure you understand the terms and conditions, including the salary, benefits, and start date. Ask for clarification if you have any questions or concerns.

Negotiate: If you are satisfied with the offer, you can negotiate the terms if you wish. For example, you can negotiate for a higher salary, flexible working hours, or additional benefits. Keep in mind that this is not always possible or feasible, and it depends on the company culture and their budget.

Consider the offer: Don't feel pressured to accept the job offer immediately. Take some time to consider the offer and whether the job and company are the right fit for you.

Get everything in writing: Once you have accepted the job offer, make sure you have a written document of the terms and conditions, including the start date, salary, benefits, and any agreements made during the negotiation.

Give notice to your current employer: If you are currently employed, give notice to your current employer through a resignation letter. Let them know that you have accepted a new job, and be professional and gracious in your communication with them. Below in an example of a resignation letter:

"[Your Name]
[Your Address]
[City, State ZIP Code]
[Your Email Address]
[Date]

[Manager's Name]
[Company Name]
[Address]
[City, State ZIP Code]

Dear [Manager's Name],

Please accept this letter as my formal resignation from my position as [Your Job Title] at [Company Name]. My last day of work will be [Date of Last Day of Work], in accordance with the notice period outlined in my contract.

I have decided to resign in order to pursue a new opportunity that aligns with my long-term career goals. I would like to express my gratitude for the opportunities and support provided to me during my time here. I am proud to have been a part of such a dynamic and successful team.

In the remaining time I have with the company, I will ensure a smooth transition of my duties and responsibilities to my successor. Please let me know how I can be of assistance to facilitate this process.

Thank you again for everything, and please let me know if there is anything else I can do to assist in the transition process.

Sincerely,
[Your Name]"

Confirm the start date: Once you've accepted the job offer and given notice to your current employer, Confirm the start date and any related information, such as orientation, trainings, or equipment that you need to have before starting.

Prepare for your first day: Start preparing for your first day on the job. This could include researching the company and its culture, familiarizing yourself with the company's products or services, and getting organized.

Remember, it's always important to take the time to review the offer and make sure it's the right fit for you, but also to be prepared and excited for the new opportunities that this job will bring!

Negotiating Salary

Negotiating salary for a new job can be a difficult task, but it's an important step in ensuring that you are being fairly compensated for your skills and experience. Here are some tips for negotiating salary for a new job:

Research the market: Research the average salary for your job title and location. This will give you a good idea of what to expect and what you should be asking for.

Be prepared: Be prepared to discuss your qualifications, experience, and the value you can bring to the company. Have specific examples of your achievements and successes that demonstrate your value.

Be honest: Be honest with yourself and with the employer about your salary requirements. Be prepared to explain why you are asking for a certain salary and how it aligns with your qualifications and experience.

Be flexible: Be flexible and open to compromise. Be prepared to negotiate the salary and benefits package and be willing to compromise on certain aspects if necessary.

Be confident: Be confident when you negotiate. Speak clearly, be assertive and be willing to walk away if the salary offered is not what you were looking for.

Listen to the employer: Listen to the employer's perspective and understand their budget and resources. Show them that you understand their point of view, and that you're willing to work with them to reach a mutually beneficial agreement.

Don't rush: Don't rush into accepting a job offer without negotiating. Take your time to think it over and to weigh the pros and cons of the offer.

Avoid discussing personal finances: Avoid discussing your personal finances during the negotiations, it's not relevant to the employer and it may make you appear less professional.

Initiating the Salary Negotiation

"I would like to express my appreciation for the offer of [Job Title] at [Company Name]. I am very excited about the opportunity to work with such a dynamic team and contribute my skills and experience to the company.

However, after careful consideration, I would like to discuss the salary offer. Based on my research and experience in the field, I believe that a salary of [Desired Salary] would be more appropriate given the responsibilities and expectations of the role.

I am confident in my ability to bring significant value to the company and contribute to its success. I believe that a salary of [Desired Salary] would not only be in line with industry standards, but also reflect my experience and qualifications.

I am open to discussing other forms of compensation, such as benefits or equity, to arrive at a mutually beneficial arrangement. I understand that the company has its own budget and constraints, but I hope we can reach a compromise that works for both parties.

Thank you for your understanding and consideration. I look forward to continuing our discussion and joining the team at [Company Name]."

Keep in mind that salary negotiations can be a delicate process, and not every employer or company culture is open to negotiation. Be respectful of their constraints and if you don't get the salary that you were looking for, you can always ask for other benefits, perks, or options such as a flexible schedule, remote work, more vacation days, etc. Remember that the goal of salary negotiation is to reach an agreement that is fair for both parties.

CHAPTER 5: FIST DAY ON THE JOB

The first day of a new job can be both exciting and nerve-wracking. Here are a few things you can do to make the most of your first day:

Arrive on time: Plan to arrive at least 10-15 minutes early. This shows your punctuality and consideration for your colleagues and employer. It also gives you time to get used to the work environment.

Dress appropriately: Make sure you're dressed appropriately for the job and company culture. This will show that you take the job seriously and that you're professional.

Bring necessary items: Bring any necessary items such as copies of your ID, references, and paperwork that you were asked to bring on your first day.

Be open and friendly: Be open to meeting new people and be friendly. Introduce yourself to your colleagues and try to remember their names.

Be ready to learn: Be prepared to learn about the company and its products, services, and mission. Also, ask about your role, responsibilities, and goals for the first weeks or months.

Ask for help: Don't be afraid to ask for help. If you need assistance or have any questions, don't hesitate to ask your colleagues or supervisor.

Take notes: Take notes during the orientation, trainings and any other information that is provided to you. This will help you to remember important information and to stay organized.

Be positive: Maintain a positive attitude and be enthusiastic about your new job. This will help you to adjust to your new environment and to make a good impression with your colleagues and employer.

Remember, the first day of a new job is an opportunity to learn, grow, and make a great impression with your new colleagues and employer. Show up ready to work, open to learn and be excited about the new opportunities that this job will bring to your life.

CHAPTER 6: BECOMING A SUCCESSFUL EMPLOYEE

Being a successful employee involves a combination of skills, attitudes, and behaviors. Here are some tips for being a successful employee:

Be punctual and reliable: Show up to work on time and be reliable. This will help you to establish a good reputation and to build trust with your colleagues and employer.

Be organized: Keep yourself and your work area organized. This will help you to stay on top of your tasks and to be more productive.

Be a good listener: Be a good listener and be open to feedback. This will help you to understand the needs of your colleagues and employer, and it will help you to improve your work.

Be a team player: Be a team player and work well with others. This will help to build good relationships with your colleagues and to achieve common goals.

Be proactive: Take initiative and be proactive. Seek out new opportunities and take on additional responsibilities. This will help you to show your value to the company and to advance your career.

Be flexible: Be flexible and adaptable to change. Be open to new ideas, processes, and technologies. This will help you to stay relevant in the job market and adapt to changes in your industry.

Communicate effectively: Communicate effectively and clearly with your colleagues, supervisors, and clients.

This will help you to build trust, avoid misunderstandings and to get things done.

Continuously improve: Continuously improve your skills and knowledge. Take courses, attend training sessions, read industry publications, and keep yourself up to date. This will help you to stay current and to achieve more in your job.

Maintain a positive attitude: Maintain a positive attitude, be resilient and stay optimistic. This will help you to overcome challenges and to maintain a good work-life balance.

By following these tips, you can develop the skills and behaviors that are needed to be a successful employee and advance in your career. Remember that success is not only achieved by individual effort but also with the support of your colleagues, superiors, and the company culture, so always strive to maintain a good relationship with all of them.

CHAPTER 7: LET'S TALK ABOUT BENEFITS

Employer benefits are additional perks or compensation beyond salary that employers offer to employees as part of their total compensation package. Here are some common types of employer benefits:

Health Insurance

Health insurance: Many employers offer health insurance as a benefit, which can help employees pay for medical expenses, including doctor visits, prescription medications, and hospital stays.

- **Preferred Provider Organization (PPO) plans:** PPO plans provide access to a network of preferred providers and allow employees to see out-of-network providers for a higher cost. PPO plans usually require co-pays for doctor visits and prescription medications.

- **Health Maintenance Organization (HMO) plans:** HMO plans require employees to choose a primary care physician and generally only cover care provided by network providers. HMO plans may have lower out-of-pocket costs and require no deductible, but may limit options for care.

- **High-Deductible Health Plans (HDHP):** HDHPs have lower monthly premiums but higher deductibles, meaning employees pay more out of pocket before insurance starts to cover costs. HDHPs may be paired with a Health Savings Account (HSA), which allows employees to save pre-tax dollars to pay for medical expenses.

- **Point of Service (POS) plans:** POS plans allow employees to choose between seeing providers within a network or paying more to see out-of-network providers. POS plans often have higher out-of-pocket costs than HMO or PPO plans.

- **Exclusive Provider Organization (EPO) plans:** EPO plans require employees to use providers within the network, like HMO plans. However, EPO plans may have more flexible options for seeing out-of-network providers in certain situations.

- **Indemnity plans:** Indemnity plans, also known as fee-for-service plans, allow employees to choose any provider and pay a portion of the cost for services. Indemnity plans may have higher out-of-pocket costs and require employees to submit claims for reimbursement.

Dental Insurance

Dental insurance is a type of insurance designed to help cover the costs of dental care, such as routine check-ups, cleanings, fillings, and other dental procedures. Like other types of insurance, individuals typically pay a monthly or annual premium to the insurance company in exchange for coverage.

Dental insurance policies vary in terms of coverage, deductibles, co-pays, and maximum benefits. Some policies may only cover basic preventive care, such as check-ups and cleanings, while others may provide more comprehensive coverage for major procedures, such as orthodontic treatment or oral surgery.

Most dental insurance plans are structured as a PPO (Preferred Provider Organization) or DHMO (Dental Health Maintenance Organization). With a PPO plan, patients have more flexibility in choosing a dentist, but may pay higher costs for out-of-network care. With a DHMO plan, patients typically choose a primary dentist from a list of providers and pay lower costs for care within the network.

It's important to review the details of a dental insurance policy to understand what is covered, what costs will be incurred by the patient, and any restrictions or limitations on coverage. Some dental plans may have waiting periods before certain procedures are covered or may limit the amount of coverage for specific services.

Vision Insurance

Vision insurance is a type of insurance that helps cover the costs of routine eye care, such as eye exams, prescription eyewear, and contact lenses. Like other types of insurance, individuals typically pay a monthly or annual premium to the insurance company in exchange for coverage.

Vision insurance policies vary in terms of coverage, deductibles, co-pays, and maximum benefits. Some policies may only cover basic preventive care, such as annual eye exams, while others may provide more comprehensive coverage for eyeglasses, contact lenses, and other vision correction options.

Most vision insurance plans are structured as a PPO (Preferred Provider Organization) or HMO (Health Maintenance Organization). With a PPO plan, patients have more flexibility in choosing an eye doctor, but may pay higher costs for out-of-network care. With an HMO plan, patients typically choose a primary eye doctor from a list of providers and pay lower costs for care within the network.

Retirement Plans

Retirement plans: Employer-sponsored retirement plans, such as 401(k) or pension plans, allow employees to save for retirement with contributions from both the employer and the employee.

401(k) plans: 401(k) plans allow employees to make pre-tax contributions from their salary, which are invested in a range of investment options offered by the plan. Employers may also offer matching contributions, up to a certain percentage of the employee's salary.

403(b) plans: 403(b) plans are similar to 401(k) plans, but are offered to employees of non-profit organizations, such as schools and hospitals.

Pension plans: Pension plans are traditional defined benefit plans that promise a set benefit amount to employees upon retirement, based on their salary and years of service. Pension plans are less common now than they were in the past.

Profit-sharing plans: Profit-sharing plans allow employers to contribute a portion of company profits to the retirement accounts of eligible employees. The amount contributed may vary from year to year, based on the company's profits.

Simplified Employee Pension (SEP) plans: SEP plans allow employers to make contributions to the individual retirement accounts (IRAs) of eligible employees. Only the employer makes contributions to the plan.

Savings Incentive Match Plan for Employees (SIMPLE) IRA plans: SIMPLE IRA plans allow both employers and employees to contribute to an IRA for each eligible employee. Employers are required to make contributions to the plan on behalf of employees.

Life and disability insurance

Life and disability insurance: Employers may offer life and disability insurance to help employees protect their families in the event of death or disability.

Employer-provided life and disability insurance are benefits that some employers offer to their employees. These benefits are designed to provide financial protection to employees in the event of unforeseen events that impact their health and ability to work.

Employer-provided life insurance is typically offered as a term life insurance policy that provides a benefit to the employee's named beneficiary in the event of their death. The benefit amount is typically based on the employee's salary and can range from one to several times their annual salary. Some employers may offer optional supplemental life insurance that the employee can purchase to increase the benefit amount.

Employer-provided disability insurance is designed to provide income replacement if an employee becomes unable to work due to a disability or illness. Disability insurance benefits are typically paid as a percentage of the employee's salary, up to a certain maximum amount. The benefit period can vary, with some policies providing short-term benefits for a few months, and others providing long-term benefits that can last for several years.

Employer-provided life and disability insurance can provide important financial protection to employees and their families in the event of unforeseen events. It's important to carefully review policy terms, costs, and coverage limits when selecting a policy and to understand how the benefit amount is calculated and paid out.

Other Benefits

Paid time off: Many employers offer paid time off for vacation, sick leave, personal days, and holidays.

Employee assistance programs: Employee assistance programs (EAPs) provide confidential counseling, referral services, and other resources to employees and their families for a range of personal and work-related issues.

Education assistance: Some employers offer tuition reimbursement or other educational assistance to employees who want to pursue additional education or training.

Commuter benefits: Employers may offer commuter benefits, such as pre-tax transportation accounts, to help employees pay for their commute to work.

Flextime and telecommuting: Some employers offer flexible work schedules or telecommuting options, which can help employees better balance work and personal commitments.

Employee discounts: Many employers offer

employee discounts on products and services, such as gym memberships, travel, or company products.

The specific types and amount of benefits vary by employer, industry, and job level. It's important to review and compare benefits packages when considering job offers or negotiating salary and benefits.

CHAPTER 8: UNDERSTANDING INCOME TAXES

Income taxes are taxes levied on the income of individuals, businesses, and other entities. In the United States, income taxes are collected by the federal government and by most state governments. Here's how income taxes work in the United States:

Determining taxable income: The first step in calculating income taxes is to determine taxable income, which is the amount of income that is subject to tax. This is done by subtracting allowable deductions and exemptions from gross income.

Filing tax returns: Taxpayers must file tax returns with the Internal Revenue Service (IRS) by April 15th of each year. The tax return reports income, deductions, credits, and other information needed to calculate the taxpayer's tax liability.

Calculating tax liability: Once the tax return is filed, the IRS calculates the taxpayer's tax liability based on their taxable income and the tax rates in effect for the tax year. Taxpayers may owe additional taxes, or they may be entitled to a refund if they overpaid their taxes.

Paying taxes: Taxpayers can pay their taxes in a variety of ways, including through employer withholding, estimated tax payments, or lump-sum payments when taxes are due.

Tax refunds and payments: Depending on the amount of taxes withheld from your paycheck and any deductions or credits you're eligible for, you may be entitled to a tax refund. If you owe more in taxes than you've already paid, you'll need to make a payment to the government to cover the difference.

Quick Guide on Doing Your Own Taxes

Gather all necessary information: You will need your W2 form, which your employer is required to provide to you by January 31st. You will also need any other tax-related documents, such as 1099 forms if you are self-employed or have other sources of income.

Determine your filing status: Your filing status will determine the tax rates and deductions you are eligible for. You can choose from single, married filing jointly, married filing separately, head of household, or qualifying widow(er).

Calculate your income: Add up all sources of income, including wages, salaries, tips, and any other taxable income.

Deduct any eligible expenses: You may be eligible for deductions, such as charitable contributions, medical expenses, or business expenses if you are self-employed.

Calculate your taxes owed: Use tax tables or tax software to determine the amount of federal and state taxes owed.

File your tax return: Submit your tax return and any required payments to the IRS by the tax filing deadline, which is usually April 15th. You can file your tax return electronically using tax software or by mail.

The tax code is complex and subject to change, and it's important for taxpayers to understand their tax obligations and take advantage of all available deductions and credits. Consulting with a tax professional can help ensure that taxpayers are properly managing their tax liabilities and maximizing their tax savings.

CHAPTER 9: CREATING A MONTHLY BUDGET

Creating a monthly budget is an important step in managing your finances and achieving your financial goals. You can create a budget using Excel or used budgeting apps. Here's how you can create a basic monthly budget:

Determine your monthly income: Calculate your total monthly income, including your salary, wages, bonuses, and any other sources of income.

List your expenses: Make a list of all your monthly expenses, including rent or mortgage payments, utilities, transportation costs, groceries, and any other recurring bills or expenses.

Categorize your expenses: Group your expenses into categories, such as housing, transportation, food, entertainment, and debt payments.

Calculate your total expenses: Add up your monthly expenses to determine your total monthly expenses.

Compare your income and expenses: Compare your total monthly income to your total monthly expenses. If your expenses are higher than your income, you may need to make some adjustments to your budget.

Identify areas to cut back: Look for areas where you can cut back on expenses. This might include reducing your entertainment expenses, finding ways to save on groceries, or negotiating lower bills with service providers.

Set goals: Set financial goals for yourself, such as paying off debt, building an emergency fund, or saving for a down payment on a house. Make sure your budget is aligned with your goals.

Track your spending: Keep track of your spending throughout the month to ensure that you're sticking to your budget. You can use a spreadsheet or budgeting app to track your spending and adjust as needed.

Remember, creating a monthly budget is just the first step in achieving your financial goals. It's important to stick to your budget, track your spending, and adjust as needed to ensure that you're on track to meet your goals.

CHAPTER 10: PAYING OFF YOUR DEBT VS SAVING

Whether to pay off debt or save is a common financial dilemma that many people face. The answer depends on your specific financial situation and goals. Here are some factors to consider when deciding whether to pay off debt or save:

Interest rates: Compare the interest rates on your debt with the potential returns on your savings. If the interest rate on your debt is higher than the potential returns on your savings, it may be more financially beneficial to focus on paying off your debt first.

Emergency fund: It's important to have an emergency fund to cover unexpected expenses, such as medical bills or car repairs. If you don't have an emergency fund, consider setting aside some money before paying off debt.

Debt type: Not all debt is created equal. High-interest debt, such as credit card debt, should be a priority to pay off quickly. However, some debt, such as a low-interest mortgage or student loan, may be more manageable to pay off over time while building savings.

Personal goals: Consider your personal goals and values. If saving for a down payment on a home or retirement is a priority, it may be better to prioritize saving. On the other hand, if being debt-free is important to you, paying off debt may be a priority.

Emotional well-being: Debt can cause stress and anxiety, and being debt-free can be a huge relief. If being debt-free will significantly improve your emotional well-being, it may be worth prioritizing paying off debt.

In general, it's important to find a balance between paying off debt and saving. Creating a plan that addresses both priorities can help you achieve your financial goals over the long-term. It's a good idea to consult with a financial advisor to determine the best course of action for your specific financial situation.

CHAPTER 11: EMERGECY FUND

The amount you should keep in your emergency fund can vary depending on your personal circumstances. Here are some factors to consider when deciding how much to keep in your emergency fund:

Living expenses: Calculate your monthly living expenses, including rent or mortgage payments, utilities, food, transportation, and other essential expenses. Aim to save enough to cover at least three to six months of living expenses.

Job stability: If you have a stable job with a steady income, you may be able to save less than someone with an unstable income or irregular work. If you have a variable income, consider saving more in your emergency fund to cover potential gaps in income.

Health: If you have health issues or dependents with medical needs, you may want to save more in your emergency fund to cover unexpected medical expenses.

Housing situation: If you own a home, you may need to save more in your emergency fund to cover unexpected home repairs or maintenance.

Insurance coverage: Check your insurance coverage, including health, disability, and homeowner or renter's insurance, to make sure you have adequate coverage. This can help you determine how much to save in your emergency fund.

In general, it's a good idea to aim for at least three to six months of living expenses in your emergency fund. However, you may want to save more depending on your personal circumstances. It's important to regularly review and adjust your emergency fund as needed to ensure that it remains adequate for your current financial situation.

CHAPTER 12: CREDIT CARDS

Using a credit card can be a good idea if you use it responsibly and within your means. Credit cards offer several benefits, such as convenience, security, and the ability to build credit history. Here are some of the advantages of using a credit card:

Convenience: Credit cards are widely accepted, and you can use them to make purchases both online and offline.

Rewards: Many credit cards offer rewards programs, such as cashback, points, or miles, which can be used to earn discounts, travel perks, and other benefits.

Security: Credit cards offer better fraud protection than debit cards or cash, and you can dispute any unauthorized charges on your account.

Building credit: Using a credit card responsibly can help you establish a good credit score, which is important if you want to qualify for loans, mortgages, or other financial products. However, it's important to use your credit card responsibly and avoid overspending. Here are some tips to keep in mind:

- Pay your balance in full every month to avoid interest charges.
- Stick to a budget and avoid using your credit card for purchases you can't afford.
- Don't carry a balance from month to month, as this can lead to high interest charges and debt.
- Choose a credit card with a low interest rate and fees.

In summary, credit cards can be a good tool to use, but it's important to use them responsibly and within your means.

CHAPTER 13: IMPORTANCE OF CREDIT SCORES

A credit score is an important financial tool that measures an individual's creditworthiness based on their credit history. It's a three-digit number that ranges from 300 to 850 and is used by lenders, landlords, insurance companies, and other organizations to evaluate a person's financial risk. Here are some reasons why having a good credit score is important:

Getting approved for loans and credit products: Lenders use credit scores to determine whether to approve a loan or credit application. A higher credit score indicates that the borrower is more likely to pay back the loan, making them a lower risk and more likely to be approved.

Getting better interest rates: A higher credit score can lead to better interest rates on loans and credit products. This can save you money over time by reducing the amount of interest you pay on your debt.

Lowering insurance premiums: Insurance companies may use credit scores to determine premiums for auto, home, or life insurance. A higher credit score can lead to lower insurance premiums, as it indicates a lower risk for the insurer.

Renting an apartment: Landlords may use credit scores to evaluate potential tenants. A good credit score can increase your chances of being approved for an apartment and may also lead to better rental terms.

Employment opportunities: Some employers may run

credit checks as part of the hiring process. A good credit score can indicate financial responsibility, which may make you a more attractive candidate for certain positions.

What Affects Your Credit Score

Several factors can affect your credit score, including:

Payment history: Payment history is the most important factor in determining your credit score. Late or missed payments can have a significant negative impact on your score.

Credit utilization: Credit utilization is the amount of credit you're using compared to your total available credit. High credit utilization can lower your score, as it suggests that you may be overextended and struggling to manage your debt.

Length of credit history: The length of time you've had credit accounts open can also affect your score. Generally, a longer credit history is seen as a positive factor, as it shows that you have a proven track record of managing credit responsibly.

Credit mix: The types of credit accounts you have can also affect your score. Having a mix of different types of credit, such as credit cards, installment loans, and a mortgage, can indicate that you have experience managing different types of debt.

New credit inquiries: Applying for new credit can

also affect your score. Each time you apply for credit, the lender will run a credit inquiry, which can temporarily lower your score.

Negative information: Bankruptcies, foreclosures, collections, and other negative information can have a significant negative impact on your score.

Increasing Your Credit Score

Improving your credit score can take time, but there are several steps you can take to help boost your score:

Pay your bills on time: Payment history is the most important factor in determining your credit score. Make sure you pay all your bills on time, including credit card payments, loan payments, and utility bills.

Reduce your credit card balances: High credit card balances can negatively impact your credit score. Try to keep your credit card balances low and pay them off in full each month if possible.

Check your credit report for errors: Check your credit report regularly and dispute any errors or inaccuracies that may be negatively impacting your score.

Don't open too many new credit accounts: Opening too many new credit accounts in a short period of time can lower your score. Only open new accounts when you need them and avoid applying for multiple accounts at once.

Keep your old credit accounts open: The length of your credit history is an important factor in determining your score. Keep old credit accounts open and active, even if you don't use them regularly.

Diversify your credit mix: Having a mix of different types of credit accounts, such as credit cards, installment loans, and a mortgage, can help boost your score.

Consider a secured credit card: If you're just starting to build credit or have a low credit score, a secured credit card may be a good option. These cards require a security deposit, but can help you establish or rebuild your credit history.

In summary, having a good credit score is important because it can help you get approved for loans and credit products, get better interest rates, lower insurance premiums, rent an apartment, and even improve your employment opportunities. It's important to maintain a good credit score by paying bills on time, keeping credit card balances low, and monitoring your credit report regularly.

It's important to monitor your credit score regularly and understand the factors that affect it. You can obtain a free credit report from each of the three major credit reporting agencies (Equifax, Experian, and TransUnion) once per year, which can help you identify any errors or issues that may be impacting your score. By managing your credit responsibly and making timely payments, you can maintain a good credit score over time.

Remember, improving your credit score takes time and effort, but it can be done with good financial habits and responsible credit management.

CHAPTER 14: UNDERSTANDING INTEREST RATES

An interest rate is the amount of money a lender charges a borrower for the use of borrowed funds. In other words, it's the cost of borrowing money.

The interest rate is usually expressed as a percentage of the loan amount or balance, and it can be fixed or variable. A fixed interest rate remains the same throughout the life of the loan, while a variable interest rate can change over time based on market conditions.

Interest rates can be applied to a variety of financial products, such as loans, credit cards, mortgages, and savings accounts. In the case of loans and credit cards, the interest rate represents the cost of borrowing money, and it's added to the amount borrowed to determine the total amount owed. For savings accounts, the interest rate represents the amount of interest earned on deposited funds.

Interest rates can vary depending on a variety of factors, such as the borrower's creditworthiness, the type of loan or credit product, the current state of the economy, and the policies of the lender or financial institution. Generally, borrowers with good credit scores and stable financial histories are offered lower interest rates, while those with poor credit or high-risk profiles may be charged higher rates.

Understanding interest rates is important when taking out loans or credit products, as it can affect the total amount owed and the monthly payments. It's important to shop around and compare rates from different lenders before making a decision to ensure you get the best deal possible.

Types of Interest Rates

Fixed rate: A fixed interest rate remains the same for the entire term of the loan or investment.

Variable rate: A variable interest rate can fluctuate over time based on changes in market conditions or other factors.

Annual percentage rate (APR): The APR is the annual rate charged for borrowing or earned from an investment, including fees and other charges.

These are just a few examples of the different types of interest rates that exist. The type of interest rate that applies to a particular loan or investment will depend on a variety of factors, including the lender, the borrower, and prevailing market conditions.

CHAPTER 15: SAVINGS ACCOUNT VS HIGH YIELD SAVINGS ACCOUNT

A **savings account** is a type of bank account that is designed for depositing and storing money. Savings accounts typically offer a lower interest rate than other types of accounts, such as checking accounts or certificates of deposit (CDs), but they offer more flexibility and easier access to your funds.

A **high-yield savings account** is a type of savings account that offers a higher interest rate than traditional savings accounts. These accounts are typically offered by online banks or credit unions, and they may require a higher minimum deposit or balance to earn the higher rate.

The main difference between a savings account and a high-yield savings account is the interest rate. High-yield savings accounts typically offer a higher rate of return, which can help your money grow faster over time. However, they may also require higher minimum balances or have other requirements to earn the higher rate.

It's important to compare the interest rates, fees, and terms of different savings accounts to find the one that best meets your needs. If you're looking to maximize your savings and earn the highest possible interest rate, a high-yield savings account may be a good option to consider.

Picking A Savings Account

Interest rate: Look for a savings account with a high annual percentage yield (APY) to earn the most interest on your savings.

Fees: Some savings accounts charge monthly maintenance fees, so look for accounts that either have no fees or low fees that you can easily avoid.

Minimum balance requirements: Some savings accounts require a minimum balance to earn interest or to avoid fees, so look for an account with a balance requirement that works for you.

FDIC insurance: Look for savings accounts that are insured by the Federal Deposit Insurance Corporation (FDIC), which protects your deposits up to $250,000 in case the bank fails.

Online access: Many savings accounts now offer online access, which can make it easier to manage your account, transfer funds, and monitor your balance.

Customer service: Look for a bank that has a reputation for good customer service and offers convenient ways to contact customer support if you have any issues.

CHAPTER 16: CHECKING ACCOUNT

A checking account is designed for day-to-day transactions and managing your daily expenses. Here are some of the most common uses for a checking account:

Depositing your income: Your paycheck can be directly deposited into your checking account, making it easy to access and manage your funds.

Paying bills: You can use your checking account to pay bills online or by writing checks. Many banks also offer bill pay services, which can help you schedule and automate your bill payments.

Withdrawing cash: You can withdraw cash from your checking account using an ATM or by visiting a bank branch.

Making purchases: You can use a debit card linked to your checking account to make purchases online or in stores.

Transferring money: You can transfer money from your checking account to other accounts, such as savings accounts, investment accounts, or other bank accounts.

Managing your budget: A checking account can help you keep track of your expenses and manage your budget by providing a record of your transactions.

It's important to use your checking account responsibly and keep track of your balance to avoid overdraft fees or other charges. Be sure to review your account statement regularly and monitor your transactions to ensure that you're staying within your budget and not overspending.

Picking A Checking Account

Fees: Look for a checking account with no monthly maintenance fees or low fees that you can easily avoid.

ATM access: Look for a checking account that offers a large network of fee-free ATMs or reimburses you for using out-of-network ATMs.

Overdraft fees: Look for a checking account that has low or no overdraft fees or offers overdraft protection to help you avoid fees.

Interest rate: Some checking accounts offer interest on your balance, so look for an account with a competitive interest rate if you plan to keep a high balance.

Mobile app and online access: Many checking accounts now offer convenient mobile apps and online access, which can make it easier to manage your account, deposit checks, and pay bills.

Customer service: Look for a bank that has a reputation for good customer service and offers convenient ways to contact customer support if you have any issues.

Ultimately, the "best" checking account will depend on your individual needs and priorities. Consider these factors and compare different options to find the checking account that works best for you.

CHAPTER 17: THE STOCK MARKET

The stock market is a place where stocks, also known as shares or equity, are bought, and sold. A stock represents ownership in a company, and when you buy a share of stock, you are essentially buying a small piece of that company. Here's how the stock market works in basic terms:

Companies issue stocks: When a company wants to raise money, it may issue stocks to the public. This means that the company is selling ownership in the company in the form of shares of stock.

Investors buy and sell stocks: Investors, such as individuals or institutions, can buy and sell shares of stock in the company on a stock exchange. The price of the stock is determined by supply and demand: if more people want to buy a stock, the price will go up, and if more people want to sell, the price will go down.

Stock prices change: The price of a stock can change rapidly based on a variety of factors, including the company's financial performance, economic conditions, industry trends, and investor sentiment.

Investors may earn returns: Investors who own stocks may earn returns in two ways: through capital appreciation (when the stock price goes up) and through dividends (when the company pays out a portion of its profits to shareholders).

Overall, the stock market provides a way for companies to raise capital and for investors to earn returns by buying and selling shares of stock. However, investing in the stock market also comes with risks, and it's important to do your research and understand the potential risks and rewards before investing.

How to Participate in the Stock Market

There are several ways to participate in the stock market. Here are some of the most common ways:

Open a brokerage account: To buy and sell stocks, you'll need to open a brokerage account with a brokerage firm. There are many online brokers available, and many of them offer low fees and easy-to-use platforms for trading stocks.

Do your research: Before you start investing in stocks, it's important to do your research and understand the risks and potential rewards. You should research the companies you're interested in investing in, as well as broader economic and market trends that could impact the stock market.

Choose your stocks: Once you've done your research, you can start choosing stocks to invest in. You can choose individual stocks, or you can invest in index funds or exchange-traded funds (ETFs), which allow you to invest in a diversified portfolio of stocks.

Place your trades: When you're ready to buy or sell stocks, you can place your trades through your brokerage account. You'll need to specify how many shares you want to buy or sell, and at what price.

Monitor your investments: Once you've invested in stocks, it's important to monitor your investments and keep up to date on news and trends that could impact the stock market. You should review your portfolio regularly and adjust as needed.

It's important to note that investing in the stock market comes with risks, and it's possible to lose money.

It's important to invest with a long-term perspective and to diversify your portfolio to help minimize risk. It's also a good idea to consult with a financial advisor or professional if you're new to investing or need help managing your portfolio.

CHAPTER 18: TYPES OF REAL ESTATE INVESTING

Real estate investing can take many forms, and here are some of the most common types:

Rental properties: This involves buying a property and renting it out to tenants. Rental income can provide a steady stream of cash flow, and the property may also appreciate in value over time.

Flipping: Flipping involves buying a property, renovating it, and selling it quickly for a profit. This type of real estate investing can be risky, as it requires careful planning, knowledge of the real estate market, and the ability to manage renovation costs.

REITs: Real Estate Investment Trusts (REITs) are companies that own and manage real estate properties, and investors can buy shares of these companies. REITs provide exposure to the real estate market and can provide income through dividends.

Real estate partnerships: This involves partnering with other investors to buy and manage a property. Each investor contributes capital and shares in the profits and losses of the investment.

Real estate crowdfunding: This is a relatively new type of real estate investing that involves pooling money from multiple investors to fund a real estate project. Crowdfunding platforms allow investors to invest in a variety of real estate projects with relatively small amounts of money.

It's important to do your research and understand the risks and potential rewards of each type of real estate investing before investing your money. Real estate investing can be complex, so it's a good idea to consult with a financial advisor or professional if you're new to real estate investing or need help managing your investments.

CHAPTER 19: STARING A BUSINESS

Types of Legal Entities

There are several types of legal entities that can be established for a business or organization, each with its own advantages and disadvantages. Here are some of the most common types:

Sole proprietorship: A sole proprietorship is a business owned and operated by a single individual. This is the simplest form of business entity and requires no formal registration or paperwork.

Partnership: A partnership is a business owned by two or more individuals who share in the profits and losses of the business. Partnerships can be general partnerships or limited partnerships.

Limited Liability Company (LLC): An LLC is a hybrid entity that combines the liability protection of a corporation with the tax benefits of a partnership. Owners of an LLC are called members and have limited liability for the company's debts and obligations.

Corporation: A corporation is a separate legal entity that is owned by shareholders. Corporations offer limited liability protection to shareholders, meaning that they are not personally responsible for the company's debts and obligations.

S Corporation: An S Corporation is a type of corporation that offers the liability protection of a corporation but is taxed like a partnership, with the profits and losses passing through to the shareholders.

Nonprofit organization: A nonprofit organization is a

type of entity that is formed for a charitable, educational, or other purpose that benefits the public. Nonprofits are exempt from federal income taxes and may be eligible for other tax benefits.

When choosing a legal entity for a business or organization, it's important to consider factors such as liability protection, tax implications, and management structure. Consulting with a lawyer or accountant can help ensure that you choose the entity that best fits your needs.

Brainstorming Business Ideas

Brainstorming new business ideas is a creative process that can be challenging. Here are some tips to help you get started:

Identify a problem to solve: Think about a problem that you or others are facing in your daily lives. Brainstorm ways that you could solve that problem with a new product or service.

Look for gaps in the market: Look for areas where there is a gap in the market or an unmet need. This could be a new product or service that doesn't currently exist, or an existing product or service that could be improved upon.

Explore your passions and skills: Consider your own passions and skills. Is there a business idea that would allow you to combine your interests and skills in a unique way?

Research trends: Keep up with current trends and industry news to identify new opportunities. Consider emerging technologies, changing consumer behaviors, and shifts in the economy.

Collaborate with others: Brainstorm with friends, family, or colleagues to generate new ideas. Sometimes, other perspectives can help you see things in a new way and spark new ideas.

Keep an open mind: Don't be afraid to think outside the box and consider unconventional ideas. Sometimes, the most successful businesses are those that take a new approach or disrupt the status quo.

Remember, the most important thing is to start generating ideas and not to be afraid to fail. Brainstorming is just the first step in the process of starting a successful business. Once you have some ideas, it's important to research, validate, and test them to see if they have potential for success.

Creating a Business Plan

Creating a business plan is an important step in starting a new business or expanding an existing one. Here are the key steps to creating a business plan:

Executive summary: This section should provide an overview of your business, including your mission statement, products or services, target market, and financial projections.

Company description: This section should provide more detail about your business, including its history, legal structure, management team, and any partnerships or collaborations.

Market analysis: This section should provide a detailed analysis of your target market, including demographics, customer needs, and competitors. It should also include information on industry trends and potential opportunities.

Products or services: This section should provide a detailed description of your products or services, including their features, benefits, and pricing.

Marketing and sales strategies: This section should describe your marketing and sales strategies, including how you plan to reach your target market and promote your products or services.

Operations plan: This section should describe how your business will operate, including your production or service delivery processes, staffing needs, and equipment requirements.

Financial projections: This section should include detailed financial projections for your business, including income statements, balance sheets, and cash flow statements.

Funding requirements: This section should describe your funding requirements, including how much capital you need and how you plan to use it.

Appendix: This section should include any additional information that supports your business plan, such as resumes of key team members, market research reports, or product samples.

When creating a business plan, be sure to tailor it to your specific business and audience. Use clear, concise language and focus on the key elements that are most important to your investors or lenders. Finally, be sure to review and update your business plan regularly to reflect changes in your business or industry.

Acquiring Business Capital

Finding capital to start a new small business can be challenging, but there are several options to consider. Here are some ways to find capital for your new small business:

Personal savings: One of the most common ways to fund a new small business is by using personal savings. This can include money from savings accounts, retirement accounts, or other investments.

Loans: There are several types of loans available for small businesses, including traditional bank loans, Small Business Administration (SBA) loans, and alternative lenders such as online lenders or peer-to-peer lending platforms. Each option has its own requirements and terms, so be sure to research your options and compare rates and fees.

Crowdfunding: Crowdfunding platforms such as Kickstarter or GoFundMe allow you to raise money from a large group of people who support your business idea. This can be a great way to generate capital while also building a community around your business.

Grants: There are several organizations that offer grants to small businesses, including government agencies, foundations, and corporations. Be sure to research grant opportunities and carefully review the requirements and eligibility criteria.

Angel investors: Angel investors are high net worth individuals who invest in early-stage startups in exchange for equity in the company. This can be a good option for businesses with high growth potential and a strong business plan.

Venture capital: Venture capital firms invest in startups with high growth potential in exchange for equity in the company. This can be a good option for businesses that are already generating revenue and have a solid growth plan.

It's important to carefully consider your options and choose the best funding source for your business. Be sure to review the terms and requirements of each option and seek advice from professionals such as attorneys or accountants if necessary.

Understanding Financial Statements

There are four main types of financial statements that are typically prepared by businesses:

Income Statement: Also known as a profit and loss statement, this financial statement shows a company's revenues, expenses, and net income (or loss) over a specific period, typically a month, quarter, or year. The income statement is used to evaluate a company's profitability and assess its ability to generate revenue.

Balance Sheet: This financial statement shows a company's assets, liabilities, and equity at a specific point in time. The balance sheet is used to evaluate a company's financial health and assess its ability to meet its financial obligations.

Cash Flow Statement: This financial statement shows a company's cash inflows and outflows over a specific period, typically a month, quarter, or year. The cash flow statement is used to evaluate a company's liquidity and assess its ability to generate cash to meet its financial obligations.

Statement of Retained Earnings: This financial

statement shows changes in a company's retained earnings over a specific period, typically a month, quarter, or year. The statement of retained earnings is used to evaluate a company's profitability and assess its ability to generate earnings for its shareholders.

Together, these financial statements provide a comprehensive view of a company's financial performance and position, and are used by investors, lenders, and other stakeholders to make informed decisions about the company's prospects.

<u>Types of Business Taxes</u>

There are several types of business taxes that companies may be required to pay, depending on the type of business entity and the nature of their operations. Here are some of the most common types of business taxes:

Federal income tax: All businesses, including sole proprietorships, partnerships, LLCs, S corporations, and C corporations, are required to pay federal income taxes on their profits. The tax rate varies based on the business entity and the amount of taxable income.

State and local income tax: In addition to federal income tax, many states and localities also impose income tax on businesses.

Self-employment tax: Sole proprietors and partners in a partnership are considered self-employed and must pay self-employment tax, which includes both Social Security and Medicare taxes.

Employment taxes: If a business has employees, it is required to pay employment taxes, including Social Security and Medicare taxes, federal unemployment tax, and state unemployment tax.

Sales tax: Most states require businesses to collect and remit sales tax on goods and services sold within the state.

Excise tax: Excise taxes are special taxes on specific goods or activities, such as alcohol, tobacco, gasoline, and air transportation.

Property tax: Businesses that own real estate or personal property may be subject to property taxes.

It's important for businesses to understand their tax obligations and ensure that they are in compliance with all applicable tax laws and regulations. Consulting with a tax professional can help ensure that businesses are properly managing their tax liabilities and taking advantage of all available deductions and credits.

Registering Your Business

The process of registering a business can vary depending on the country/State and type of business entity. Here are some general steps you can take to register your business:

Choose a business structure: The first step in registering your business is to choose a legal structure, such as sole proprietorship, partnership, limited liability company (LLC), or corporation.

Choose a business name: Choose a name that is unique and not already taken by another business. Check with your local business registry to ensure the name is available and complies with any naming regulations.

Register with the government: You will need to register your business with the government to obtain any necessary licenses and permits, and to comply with tax and other regulatory requirements. Depending on your location, this may involve registering with your local government, state/provincial government, or federal government.

Obtain any necessary licenses and permits: Depending on your type of business and location, you may need to obtain various licenses and permits, such as a business license, tax registration, zoning permit, health permit, or environmental permit.

Register for taxes: You will need to register with the appropriate tax authorities to obtain any necessary tax identification numbers and to comply with tax requirements.

Obtain any necessary business insurance: Depending on your type of business, you may need to obtain various types of insurance, such as liability insurance, property insurance, or workers' compensation insurance.

Open a business bank account: Open a separate bank account for your business to keep your personal and business finances separate.

It's important to research and follow the specific registration requirements for your location and business type. Consult with an attorney or accountant for professional guidance and assistance with the registration process.

CHAPTER 20: PURCHASING A VEHICLE

What to Look for When Purchasing a New Car

When purchasing a new car, here are some key things to consider:

Budget: Determine how much you can afford to spend on a new car, considering not just the purchase price, but also ongoing costs such as insurance, maintenance, and fuel.

Needs: Consider your needs and lifestyle when choosing a car. Factors to consider include the number of passengers you typically carry, the amount of cargo space you need, and the type of driving you do (city vs highway, short vs long distances, etc.).

Safety: Look for a car with good safety features, such as airbags, anti-lock brakes, and electronic stability control. Check the car's safety ratings from organizations such as the National Highway Traffic Safety Administration (NHTSA) and the Insurance Institute for Highway Safety (IIHS).

Fuel efficiency: Choose a car with good fuel efficiency to save money on gas and reduce your environmental impact. Look for cars with high miles per gallon (mpg) ratings and consider hybrid or electric models.

Reliability: Look for a car with a good reputation for reliability to minimize maintenance and repair costs. Check reliability ratings from organizations such as Consumer Reports and J.D. Power.

Features: Consider the features you want in a car, such as a sunroof, heated seats, navigation system, and backup camera. However, keep in mind that more features can also mean a higher price tag.

Test drive: Always test drive a car before purchasing to ensure it feels comfortable and meets your needs. Take the car on a variety of roads and in different driving conditions to get a good sense of how it performs.

What to Look for When Purchasing a Used Car

When purchasing a used car, here are some key things to consider:

Budget: Determine how much you can afford to spend on a used car, considering not just the purchase price, but also ongoing costs such as insurance, maintenance, and repairs.

History report: Obtain a vehicle history report to check the car's accident history, ownership history, and maintenance records. You can obtain a vehicle history report from services such as Carfax or AutoCheck.

Mileage: Consider the car's mileage, as high mileage may indicate more wear and tear on the car. However, a well-maintained car with high mileage may still be a good option.

Condition: Inspect the car's exterior and interior for any signs of damage or wear and tear. Check for any rust, dents, or scratches on the exterior, and check for any stains or tears on the interior. Consider having a professional mechanic inspect the car to identify any potential issues.

Service history: Check the car's service history to see if it has been well-maintained and serviced regularly. Look for any signs of neglect, such as overdue oil changes or skipped maintenance tasks.

Test drive: Always test drive a used car before purchasing to ensure it feels comfortable and meets your needs. Take the car on a variety of roads and in different driving conditions to get a good sense of how it performs.

Warranty: Consider purchasing a warranty for the used car to protect yourself against unexpected repairs. Some dealerships may offer a limited warranty, or you can purchase an extended warranty from a third-party provider.

By considering these factors, you can find a used car that meets your needs and fits your budget while avoiding potential issues and costly repairs.

CHAPTER 21: LOOKING FOR AN APARTMENT

Looking for a new apartment can be a daunting task, but with proper planning and research, the process can be more manageable. Here are some steps you can take to look for a new apartment:

Determine your budget: Before you start looking for apartments, determine how much you can afford to spend on rent each month. Make sure to consider other expenses such as utilities, transportation, and groceries.

Decide on your preferred location: Consider factors such as proximity to work, schools, public transportation, and amenities like parks, grocery stores, and restaurants. Research different neighborhoods and determine which ones would be the best fit for you.

Start your search: Use online apartment search websites, such as Zillow or Apartments.com, to browse apartments that fit your criteria. You can also work with a real estate agent to help you find a suitable apartment.

Schedule visits: Once you have a list of apartments you are interested in, schedule visits to see them in person. Take note of the condition of the apartment, the building, and the neighborhood during your visit.

Ask questions: During your visit, ask the landlord or property manager about any concerns you may have, such as the lease terms, amenities, or any maintenance issues. Make sure you fully understand the lease before signing it.

Apply for the apartment: If you find an apartment you like, fill out the application and provide the required documents, such as your credit report and proof of income.

Prepare for move-in: Once you are approved for the apartment, start preparing for move-in day. Make a list of what you need to pack and purchase and coordinate with the landlord to schedule move-in and obtain keys.

Remember to take your time and thoroughly research each apartment before deciding. Don't rush into anything and make sure you feel comfortable with the lease terms and the condition of the apartment before signing.

CHAPTER 22: MENTAL HEALTH

Mental health refers to a person's emotional, psychological, and social well-being. It encompasses a broad range of factors that affect a person's mental and emotional state, including how they think, feel, and behave. Mental health is an important aspect of overall health and well-being, and it can be impacted by a variety of factors, such as genetics, life experiences, and environmental factors.

Good mental health involves a sense of self-worth, the ability to manage stress and emotions, and the ability to form and maintain healthy relationships. Poor mental health, on the other hand, can lead to mental illnesses such as anxiety, depression, bipolar disorder, schizophrenia, and other conditions that affect a person's thoughts, feelings, and behaviors.

It's important to note that mental health is not just the absence of mental illness, but rather a state of well-being in which an individual can cope with the normal stresses of life, work productively, and contribute to their community. Maintaining good mental health requires taking care of oneself physically, emotionally, and socially, and seeking professional help when needed.

<u>Mental Health Tips</u>

Here are some tips for improving mental health:

Practice self-care: Take time to care for your physical and emotional needs, including getting enough sleep, eating a healthy diet, engaging in regular exercise, and taking breaks when needed.

Manage stress: Learn healthy coping strategies for managing stress, such as meditation, deep breathing, and yoga. You can also try activities like spending time in nature, journaling, or spending time with loved ones to help reduce stress.

Develop healthy relationships: Nurture supportive relationships with family and friends. Having a positive social support system can help reduce feelings of loneliness, depression, and anxiety.

Seek help when needed: Don't be afraid to seek help from a mental health professional if you're struggling with your mental health. A therapist or counselor can help you develop coping strategies, manage symptoms, and provide support.

Practice mindfulness: Mindfulness is the practice of being present in the moment, without judgment. You can practice mindfulness through meditation, breathing exercises, or simply by being fully present in the activities you engage in throughout the day.

Engage in activities that bring you joy: Pursue hobbies or activities that you enjoy and that bring you a sense of fulfillment. This can help boost your mood and increase feelings of happiness and well-being.

Set realistic goals: Setting realistic and achievable goals can help give you a sense of purpose and direction in life. When setting goals, make sure they align with your values and are attainable.

Remember, taking care of your mental health is just as important as taking care of your physical health. By incorporating these tips into your daily routine, you can improve your mental health and overall well-being.

CHAPTER 23: PHYSICAL HEALTH

Physical health refers to the state of the body's overall health and well-being. It encompasses several different aspects, including the absence of disease or injury, the ability to perform daily activities and maintain physical fitness, and having a healthy balance of nutrients in the body.

Physical health is achieved through a combination of lifestyle choices, including eating a healthy diet, exercising regularly, getting enough sleep, avoiding harmful behaviors such as smoking or drug abuse, and receiving regular medical check-ups.

Good physical health not only allows an individual to perform daily tasks and activities with ease, but it also has many long-term benefits, such as reducing the risk of chronic diseases such as heart disease, stroke, diabetes, and cancer.

Maintaining good physical health requires a commitment to healthy lifestyle choices and regular medical care. Regular exercise, a healthy diet, and adequate rest and sleep are all essential for optimal physical health. It's also important to avoid risky behaviors such as smoking or drug use, and to receive regular medical check-ups to monitor and manage any potential health concerns.

Simple Workout Plans

Here are some simple workout plans for the entire

body:

Bodyweight Squats: Stand with your feet shoulder-width apart, and squat down as if sitting on an imaginary chair, keeping your chest up and knees behind your toes. Do 3 sets of 10-12 reps.

Push-ups: Place your hands on the floor shoulder-width apart, and your toes on the ground, and perform a push-up, lowering your chest towards the floor while keeping your body straight. Do 3 sets of 10-12 reps.

Plank: Place your forearms on the floor and hold your body straight, with your toes on the ground. Hold the position for 30-60 seconds, then rest and repeat for 3-4 sets.

Lunges: Stand with your feet hip-width apart, step one foot forward, and bend both knees, keeping your back straight. Push back up and repeat on the other leg. Do 3 sets of 10-12 reps on each leg.

Standing Dumbbell Shoulder Press: Hold a pair of dumbbells at shoulder height, with your palms facing forward, and press them upwards until your arms are fully extended. Lower the dumbbells back down and repeat for 3 sets of 10-12 reps.

Bent Over Dumbbell Rows: Hold a pair of dumbbells with your arms hanging straight down, then bend forward at the waist and lift the dumbbells towards your chest, keeping your elbows close to your body. Lower the dumbbells back down and repeat for 3 sets of 10-12 reps.

Remember to warm up properly before starting your workout, and to stretch and cool down after your workout. Gradually increase the intensity of your workout as you become stronger and consider working with a certified personal trainer to develop a more customized workout plan.

CHAPTER 24: NUTRITION

Good nutrition refers to consuming a balanced diet that provides the body with the necessary nutrients for optimal health and well-being. This includes a variety of foods from different food groups in appropriate proportions.

A healthy and balanced diet should include:

Fruits and vegetables: These provide essential vitamins, minerals, fiber, and antioxidants that help to protect the body from diseases.

Whole grains: These are a good source of complex carbohydrates, fiber, and vitamins and minerals that are important for energy production, digestive health, and overall well-being.

Lean proteins: These are necessary for building and repairing tissues in the body and maintaining a healthy immune system. Good sources of lean protein include chicken, fish, beans, and nuts.

Healthy fats: These are important for brain health, hormone regulation, and energy production. Sources of healthy fats include avocado, nuts, seeds, and fatty fish like salmon.

Water: Drinking enough water is important for staying hydrated and maintaining proper bodily functions.

On the other hand, a diet that is high in saturated fats, added sugars, and processed foods can increase the risk of chronic diseases such as heart disease, diabetes, and obesity.

Eating a variety of nutrient-dense foods in

appropriate portions, staying hydrated, and avoiding excessive consumption of processed and unhealthy foods are key components of a healthy and balanced diet.

FINAL THOUGHTS

I would like to share some final thoughts with you.

The main reason I wrote this book is to provide a detailed outline on how to navigate life as a younger person. These are important things in our lives that traditional education does not focus on. This book will not give all the information in the world, but you can use it as a guide to point you in the right direction.

ABOUT THE AUTHOR

Nyasha Chitakure is an entrepreneur, educator, and investor who believes in the democratization of information. Nyasha has created multiple courses and is the author of *The Age of Internet Money: Making Money Online Simplified, The Fundamental Dividend Genius: An Introduction to Dividend Investing in the Stock Market and What They Never Taught Us: The Miseducation of The Modern-Day* *Student.*

www.ingramcontent.com/pod-product-compliance
Lightning Source LLC
Chambersburg PA
CBHW070800220526
45467CB00017B/578